CHRISTMAS HITS
FOR BANJO

Banjo arrangements by Mark Switzer
and Jim Schustedt

ISBN 978-1-4950-9657-0

HAL•LEONARD®
7777 W. BLUEMOUND RD. P.O. BOX 13819 MILWAUKEE, WI 53213

Visit Hal Leonard Online at
www.halleonard.com

Blue Christmas

Words and Music by Billy Hayes and Jay Johnson

G tuning:
(5th - 1st) G-D-G-B-D

Key of C

Slow

Verse

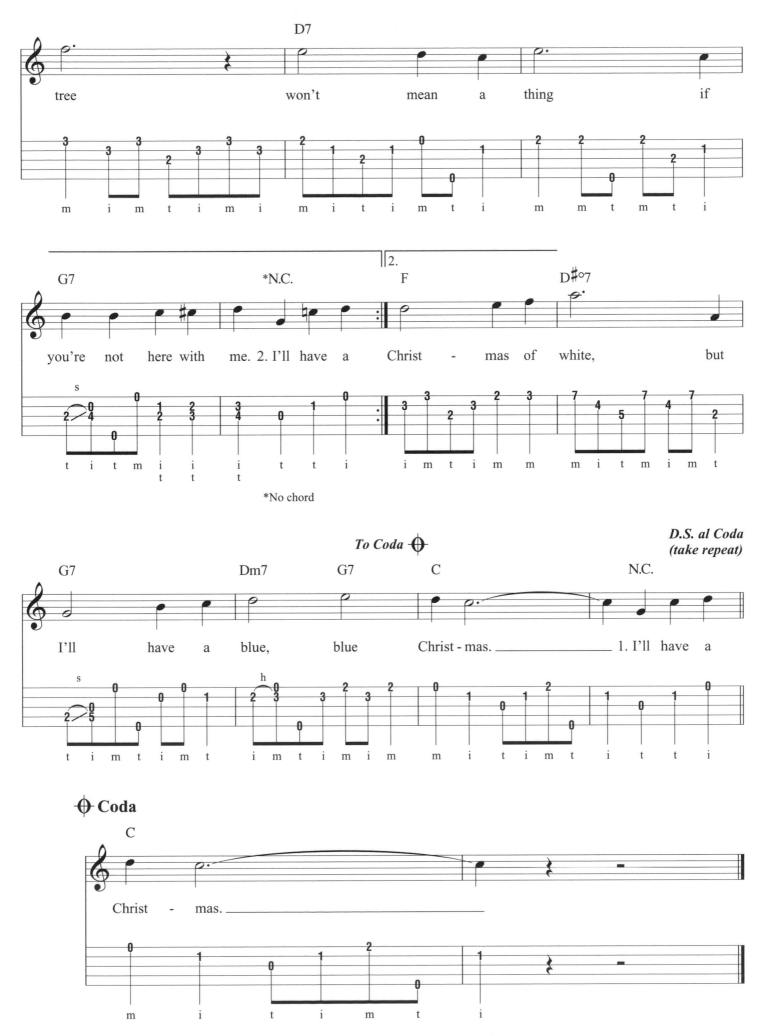

Caroling, Caroling

Words by Wihla Hutson
Music by Alfred Burt

G tuning:
(5th - 1st) G-D-G-B-D

Key of G
Verse
Moderately

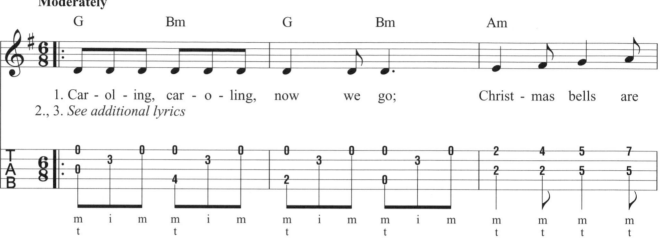

1. Car - ol - ing, car - o - ling, now we go; Christ - mas bells are
2., 3. *See additional lyrics*

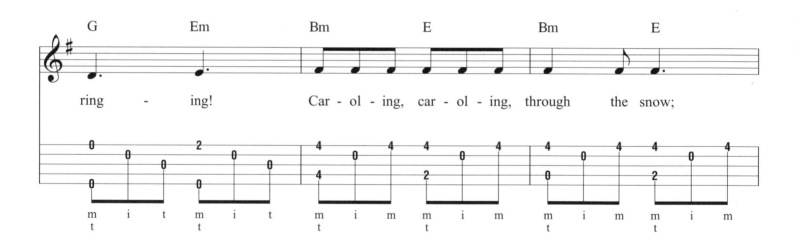

ring - ing! Car - ol - ing, car - ol - ing, through the snow;

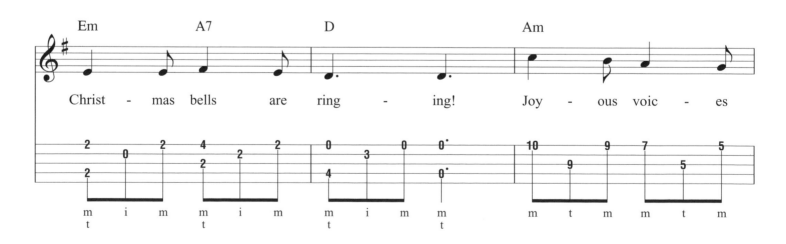

Christ - mas bells are ring - ing! Joy - ous voic - es

TRO - © Copyright 1954 (Renewed) and 1957 (Renewed) Hollis Music, Inc., New York, NY
International Copyright Secured
All Rights Reserved Including Public Performance For Profit
Used by Permission

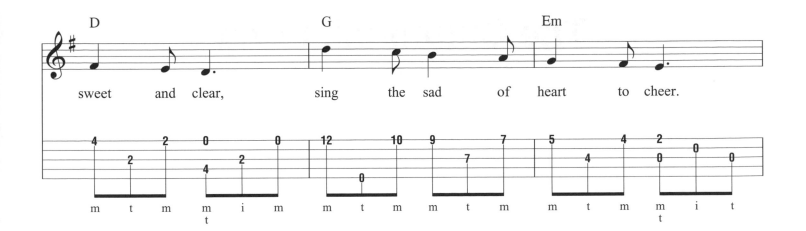

sweet and clear, sing the sad of heart to cheer.

Ding, dong, ding, dong, Christ - mas bells are ring - ing!

Additional Lyrics

2. Caroling, caroling, through the town;
   Christmas bells are ringing!
   Caroling, caroling, up and down;
   Christmas bells are ringing!
   Mark ye well the song we sing,
   Gladsome tidings now we bring.
   Ding, dong, ding, dong,
   Christmas bells are ringing!

3. Caroling, caroling, near and far;
   Christmas bells are ringing!
   Following, following yonder star;
   Christmas bells are ringing!
   Sing we all this happy morn,
   "Lo, the King of heav'n is born!"
   Ding, dong, ding, dong,
   Christmas bells are ringing!

The Chipmunk Song

Words and Music by Ross Bagdasarian

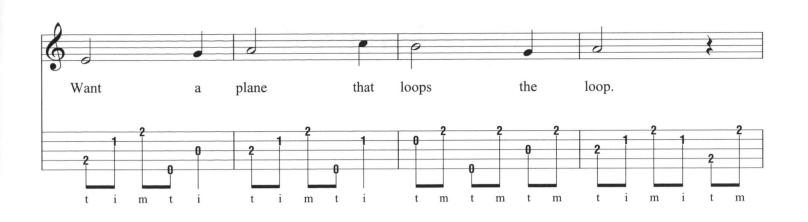

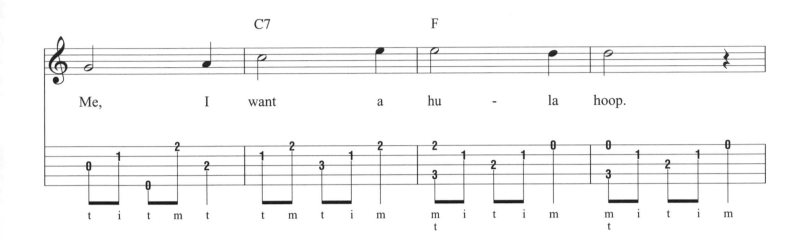

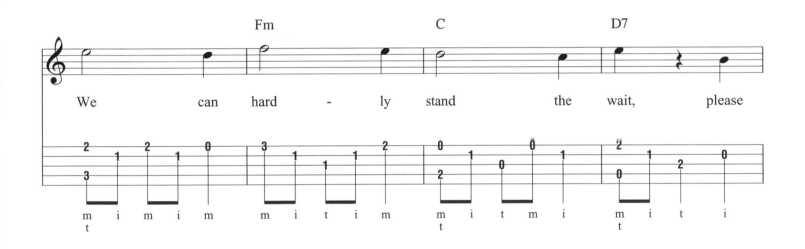

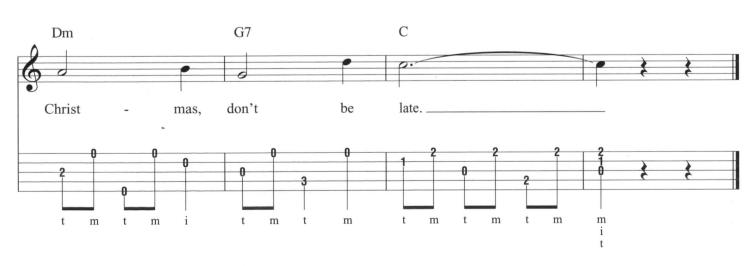

Feliz Navidad

Music and Lyrics by José Feliciano

Gmaj7 tuning:
(5th - 1st) F#-D-G-B-D

Key of D

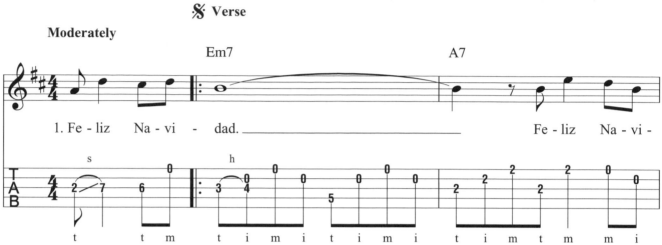

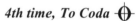

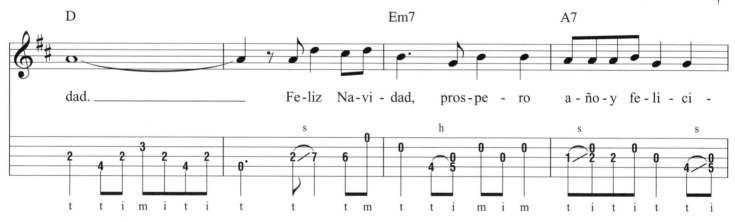

Frosty the Snow Man

Words and Music by Steve Nelson and Jack Rollins

G tuning:
(5th - 1st) G-D-G-B-D

Key of G

Verse
Brightly

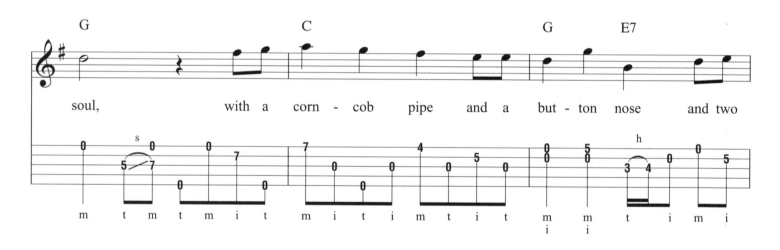

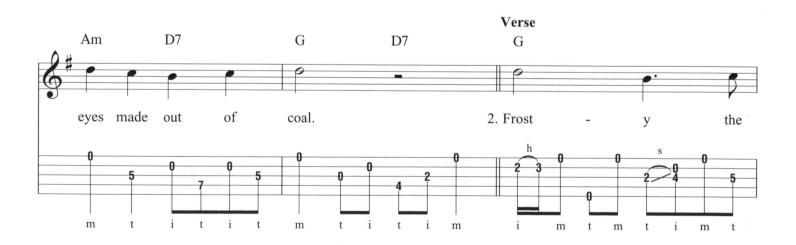

The Christmas Song

(Chestnuts Roasting on an Open Fire)

Music and Lyric by Mel Torme and Robert Wells

G tuning:
(5th - 1st) G-D-G-B-D

Key of C

Verse

Slow

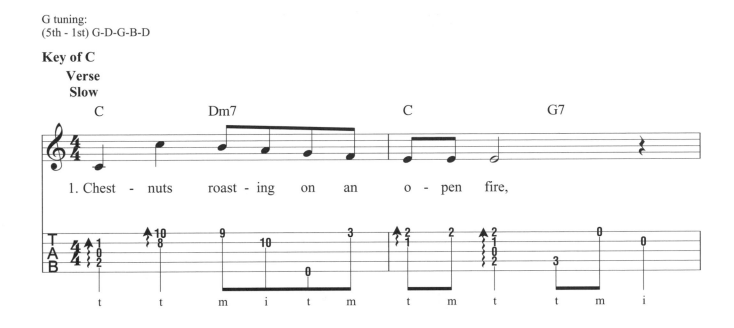

1. Chest - nuts   roast - ing   on   an   o - pen   fire,

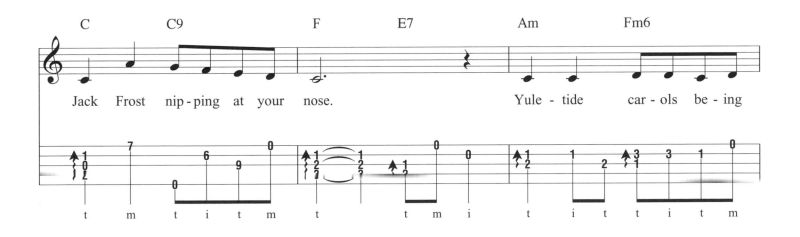

Jack Frost nip - ping at your nose.   Yule - tide   car - ols be - ing

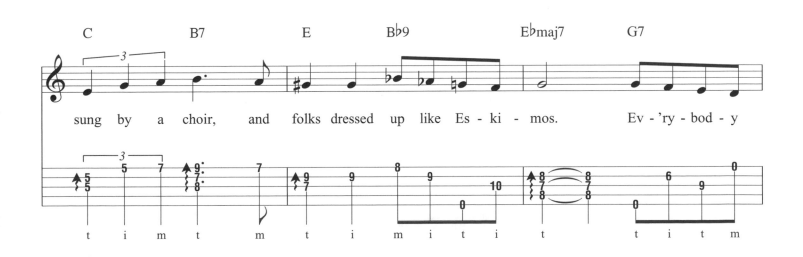

sung by a choir, and folks dressed up like Es - ki - mos.   Ev - 'ry - bod - y

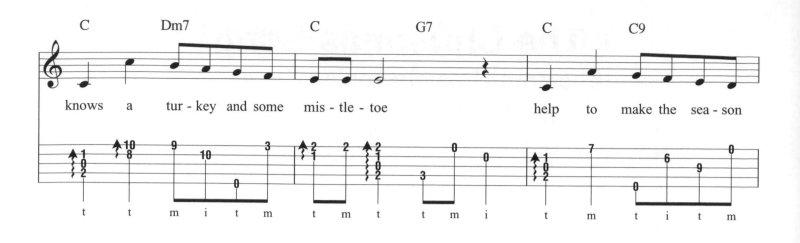

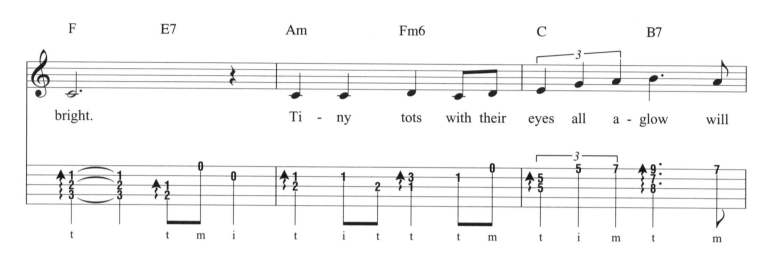

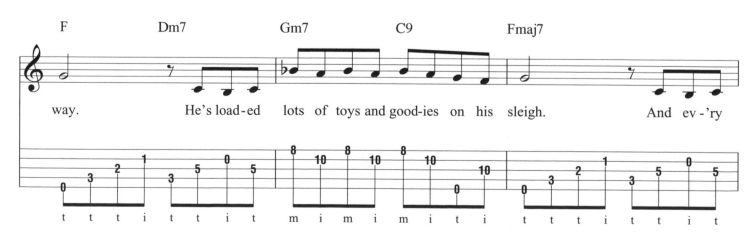

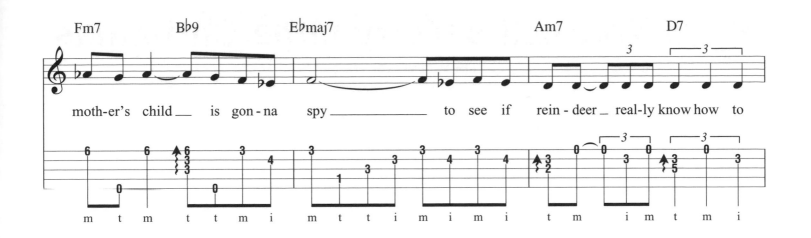

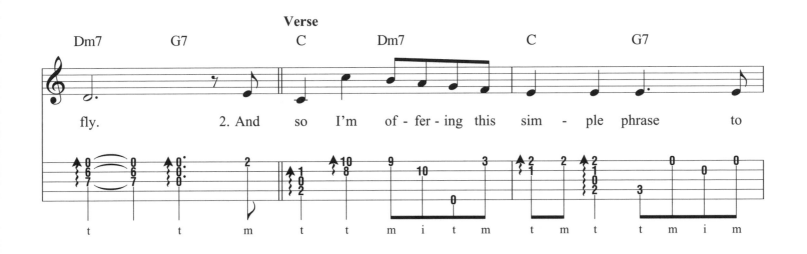

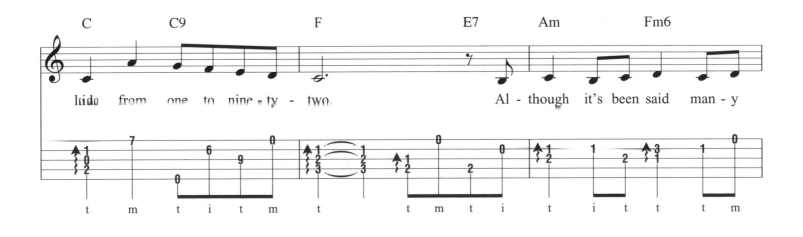

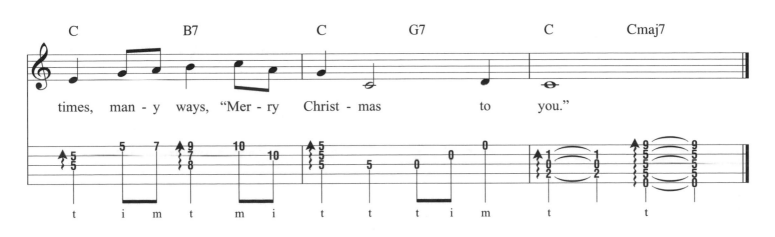

Have Yourself a Merry Little Christmas

from MEET ME IN ST. LOUIS

Words and Music by Hugh Martin and Ralph Blane

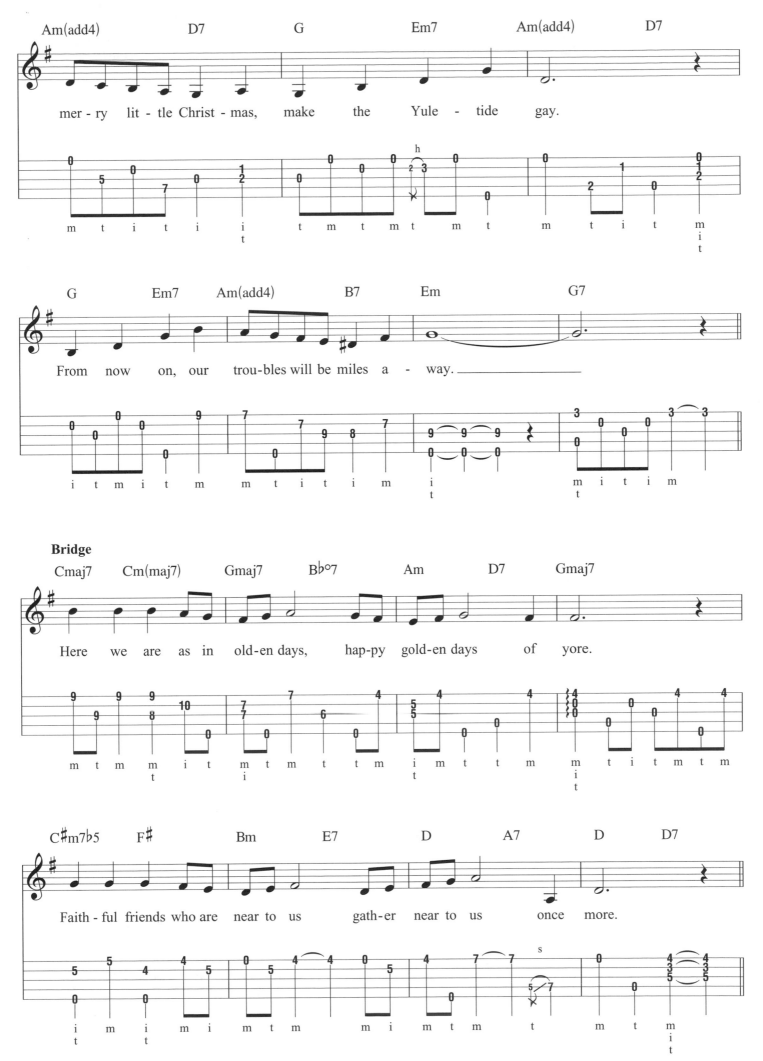

Happy Holiday

from the Motion Picture Irving Berlin's HOLIDAY INN
Words and Music by Irving Berlin

G6 tuning:
(5th - 1st) E-D-G-B-D

Key of G

Verse

Moderately

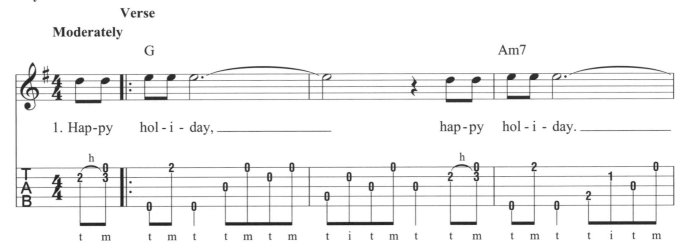

1. Hap-py hol-i-day, _____ hap-py hol-i-day. _____

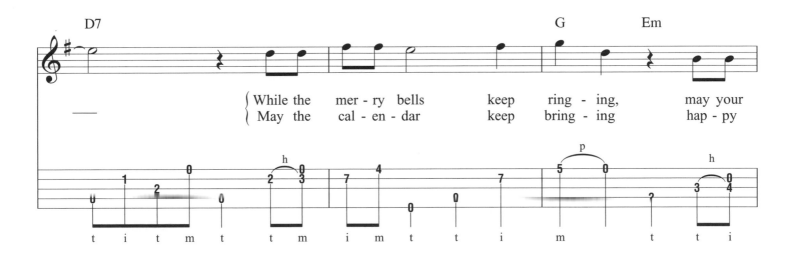

While the mer-ry bells keep ring-ing, may your
May the cal-en-dar keep bring-ing hap-py

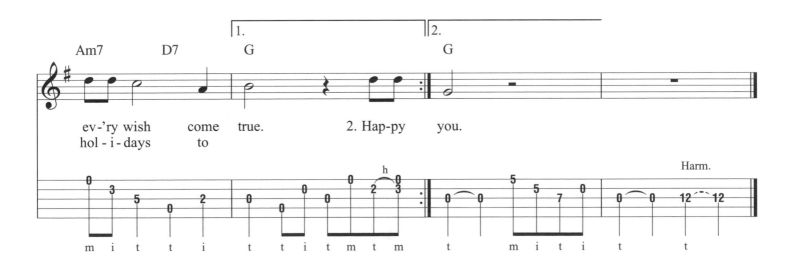

ev-'ry wish come true. 2. Hap-py you.
hol-i-days to

Here Comes Santa Claus
(Right Down Santa Claus Lane)

Words and Music by Gene Autry and Oakley Haldeman

G tuning:
(5th - 1st) G-D-G-B-D

Key of C

Verse

Moderately, in 2

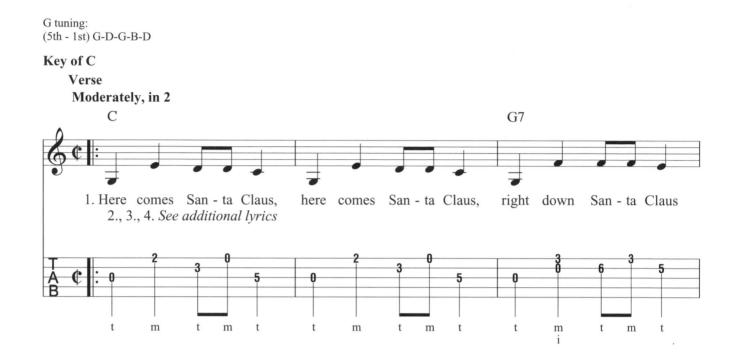

1. Here comes San - ta Claus, here comes San - ta Claus, right down San - ta Claus
2., 3., 4. *See additional lyrics*

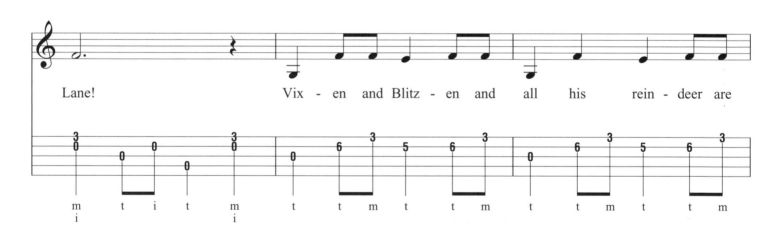

Lane! Vix - en and Blitz - en and all his rein - deer are

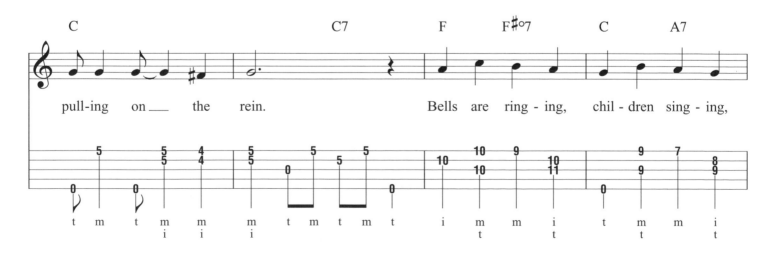

pull-ing on ___ the rein. Bells are ring - ing, chil - dren sing - ing,

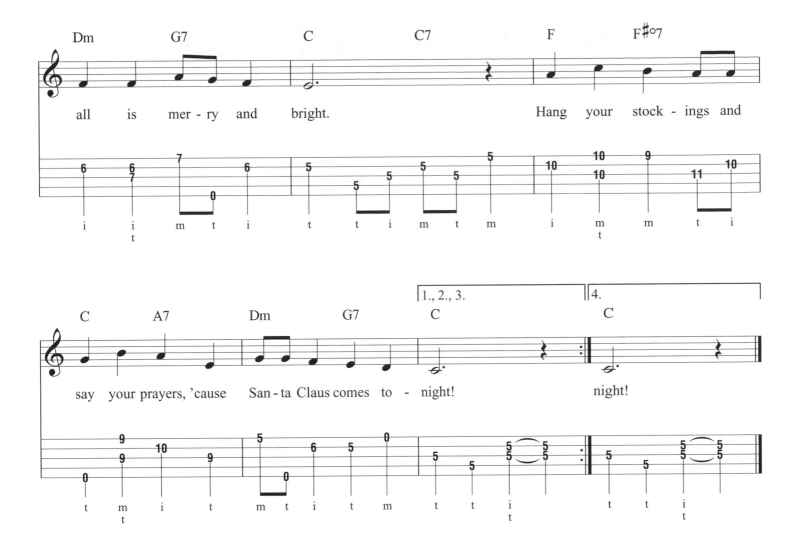

2. Here comes Santa Claus, here comes Santa Claus,
   Right down Santa Claus Lane!
   He's got a bag that is filled with toys
   For the boys and girls again.
   Hear those sleigh bells jingle, jangle,
   What a beautiful sight.
   Jump in bed, cover up your head,
   Santa Claus comes tonight!

3. Here comes Santa Claus, here comes Santa Claus,
   Right down Santa Claus Lane!
   He doesn't care if you're rich or poor,
   For he loves you just the same.
   Santa knows that we're God's children;
   That makes ev'rything right.
   Fill your hearts with a Christmas cheer,
   'Cause Santa Claus comes tonight!

4. Here comes Santa Claus, here comes Santa Claus,
   Right down Santa Claus Lane!
   He'll come around when the chimes ring out;
   Then it's Christmas morn again.
   Peace on earth will come to all,
   If we just follow the light.
   Let's give thanks to the Lord above,
   Santa Claus comes tonight!

A Holly Jolly Christmas

Music and Lyrics by Johnny Marks

G tuning:
(5th - 1st) G-D-G-B-D

Key of G

Verse

Moderately

1. Have a hol - ly jol - ly Christ-mas, it's the best time of the

year. I don't know if there'll be snow but have a cup of

cheer. Have a hol - ly jol - ly Christ-mas, and when you walk down the

street, say hel - lo to friends you know and ev - 'ry - one you

(There's No Place Like)
Home for the Holidays

Words and Music by Al Stillman and Robert Allen

G tuning:
(5th - 1st) G-D-G-B-D

Key of G

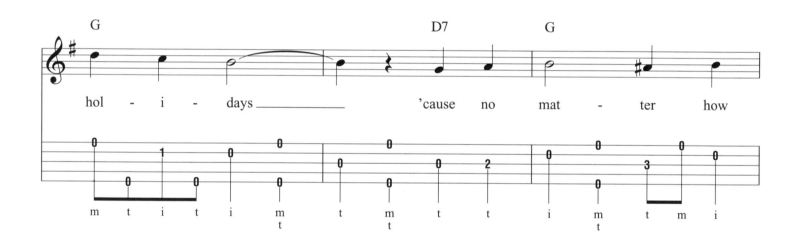

Chorus

Moderately

Oh, there's no place like home for the hol-i-days _____ 'cause no mat-ter how

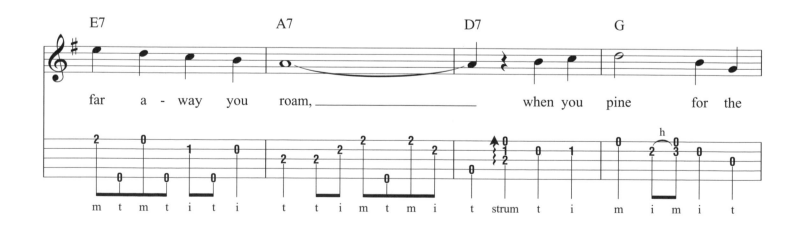

far a-way you roam, _____ when you pine for the

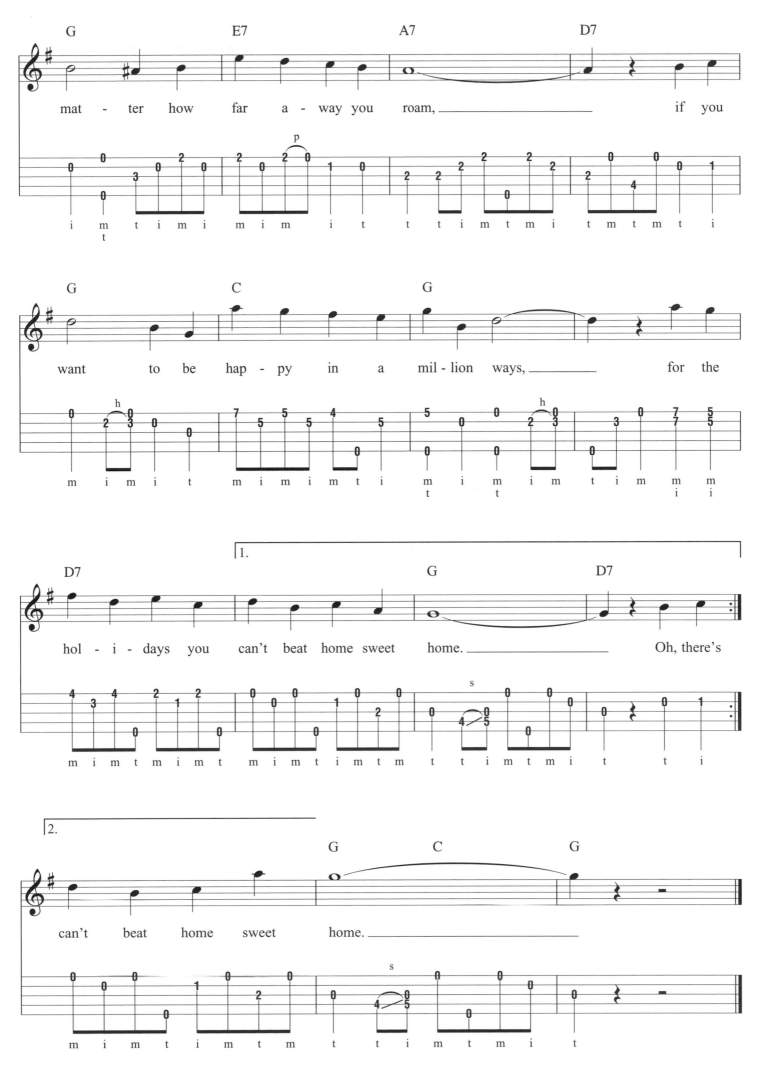

I Saw Mommy Kissing Santa Claus

Words and Music by Tommie Connor

It's Beginning to Look Like Christmas

By Meredith Willson

G tuning:
(5th - 1st) G-D-G-B-D

Key of G

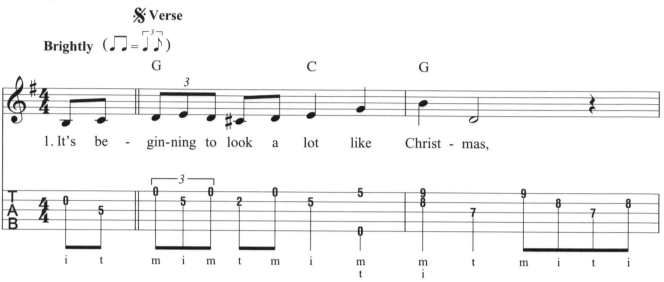

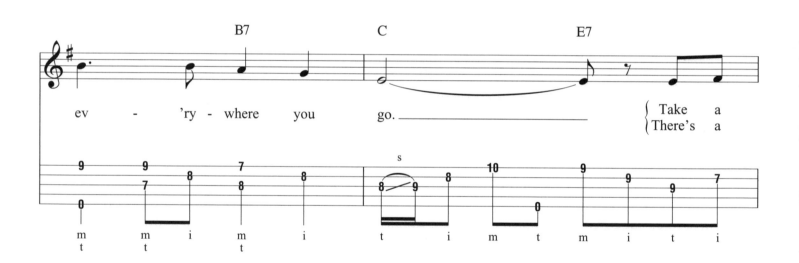

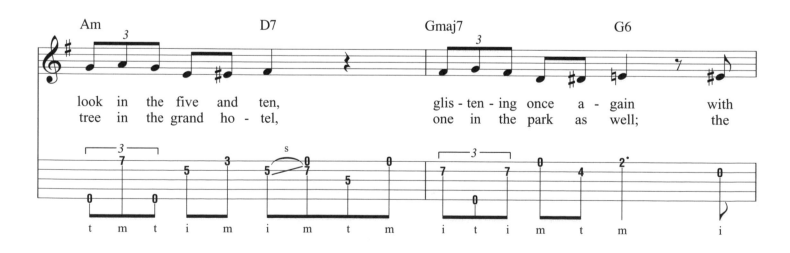

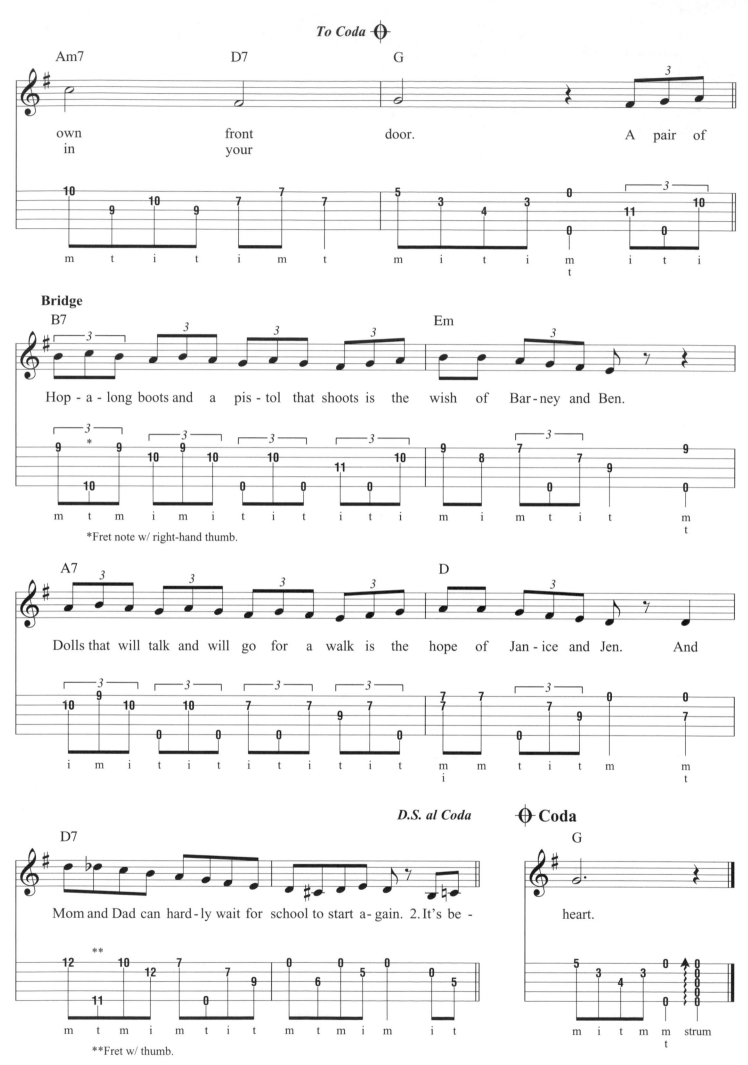

I'll Be Home for Christmas

Words and Music by Kim Gannon and Walter Kent

G tuning:
(5th - 1st) G-D-G-B-D

Key of C

Intro

Freely

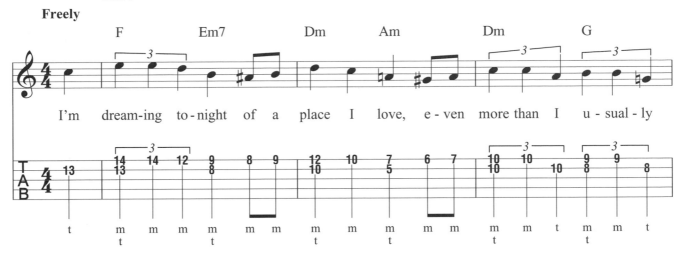

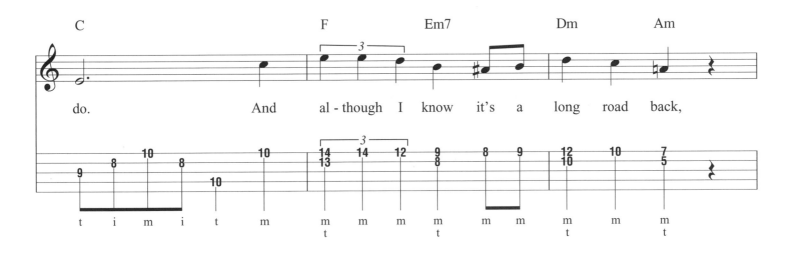

Verse
Moderately slow

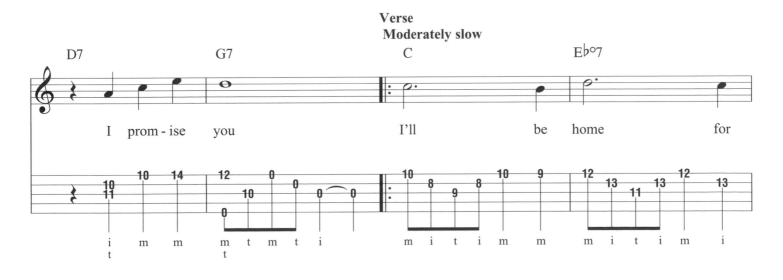

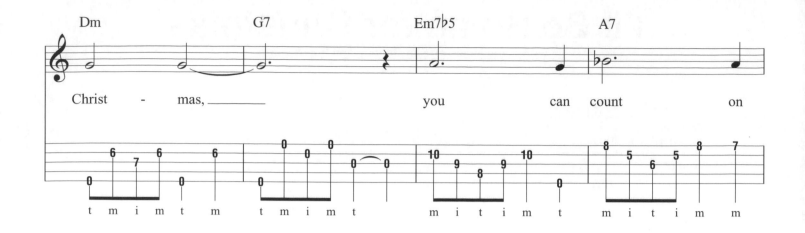

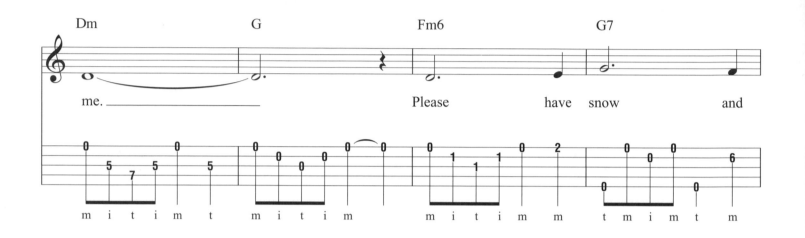

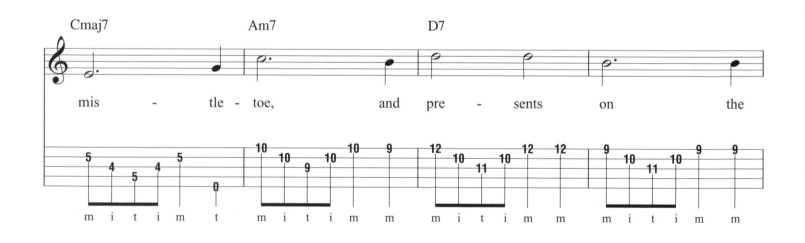

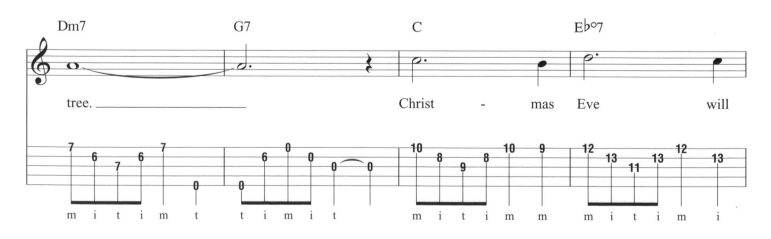

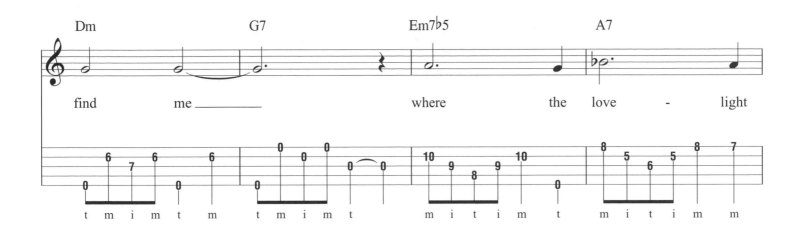

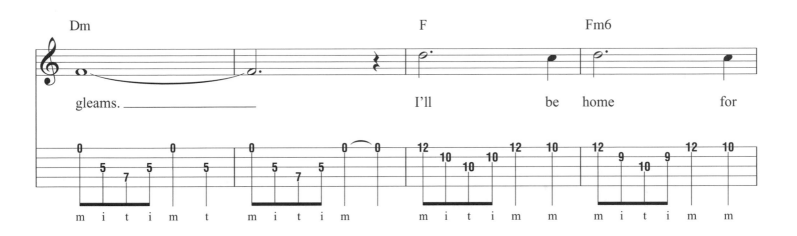

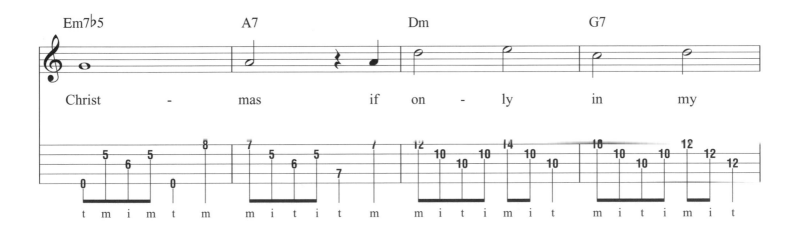

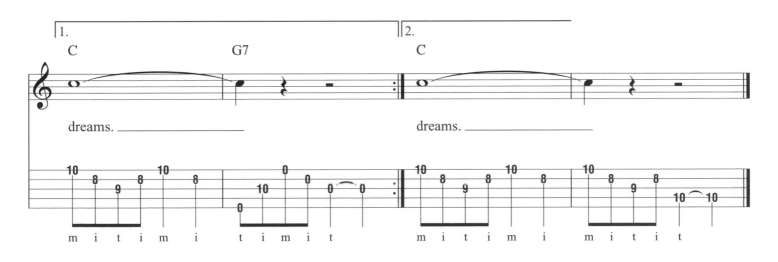

Jingle Bell Rock

Words and Music by Joe Beal and Jim Boothe

Verse

2., 4. Gid - dy - ap, jin - gle horse, pick up your feet. Jin - gle a - round the

clock. Mix and min - gle in a jin - gl - in' beat.

1.
That's the jin - gle bell rock.

2.
That's the jin - gle bell,

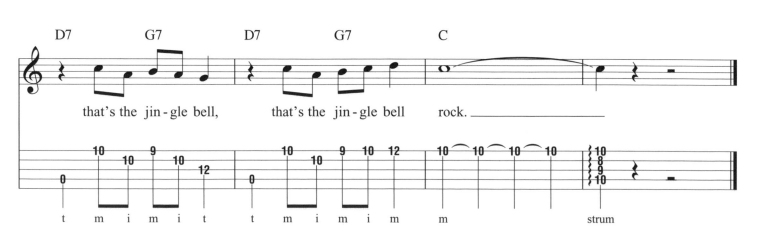

that's the jin - gle bell, that's the jin - gle bell rock. _____

The Little Drummer Boy

Words and Music by Harry Simeone, Henry Onorati and Katherine Davis

G tuning:
(5th - 1st) G-D-G-B-D

Key of G
Verse
Moderately

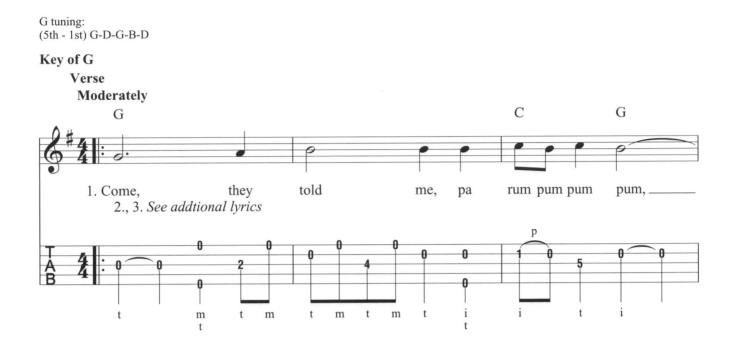

1. Come,   they   told   me, pa   rum pum pum   pum,
2., 3. *See addtional lyrics*

— our   new - born   King   to   see, pa

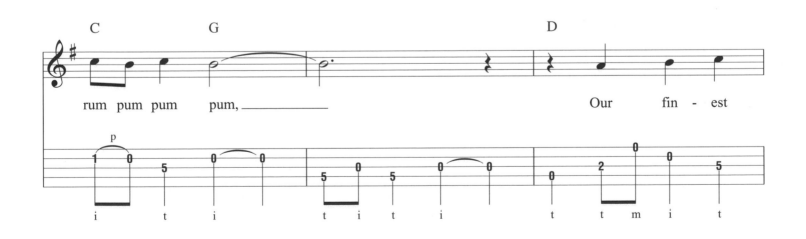

rum pum pum   pum,   Our   fin - est

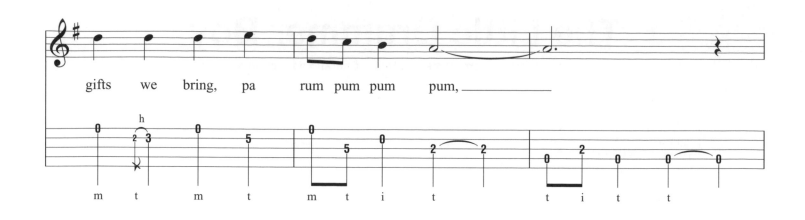

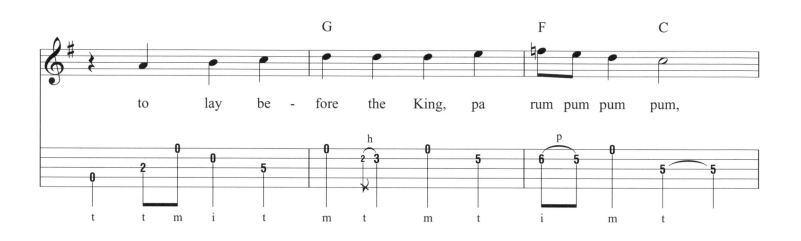

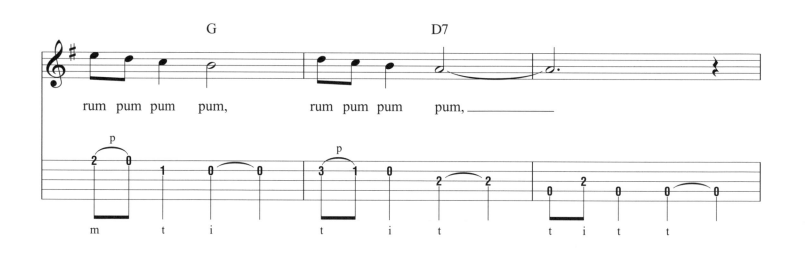

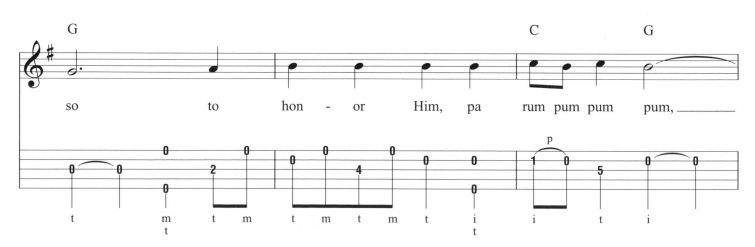

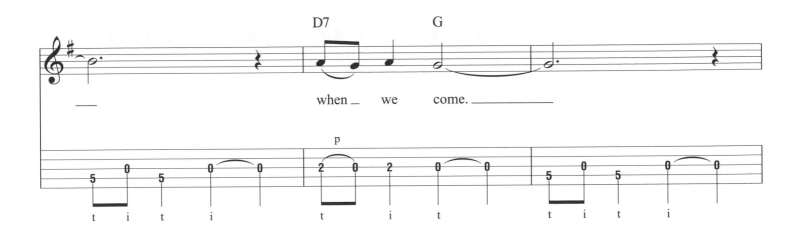

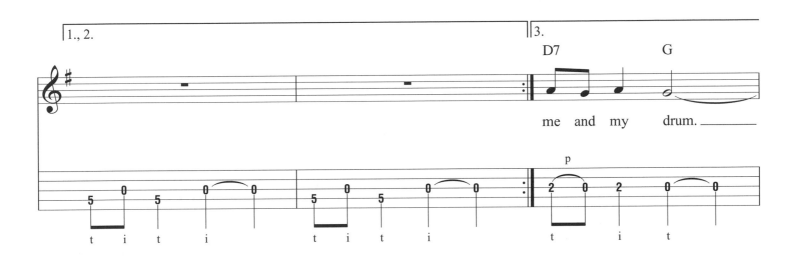

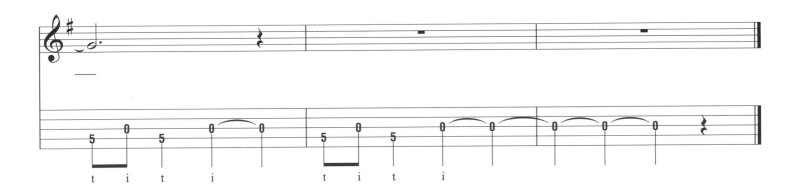

Additional Lyrics

2. Baby Jesus, pa rum pum pum pum,
  I am a poor boy too, pa rum pum pum pum.
  I have no gift to bring, pa rum pum pum pum,
  That's fit to give our King, pa rum pum pum pum,
  Rum pum pum pum, rum pum pum pum.
  Shall I play for You, pa rum pum pum pum,
  On my drum?

3. Mary nodded, pa rum pum pum pum,
  The ox and lamb kept time, pa rum pum pum pum.
  I played my drum for Him, pa rum pum pum pum,
  I played my best for Him, pa rum pum pum pum,
  Rum pum pum pum, rum pum pum pum.
  Then He smiled at me, pa rum pum pum pum,
  Me and my drum, me and my drum.

Let It Snow! Let It Snow! Let It Snow!

Words by Sammy Cahn
Music by Jule Styne

G tuning:
(5th - 1st) G-D-G-B-D

Key of G

Moderately

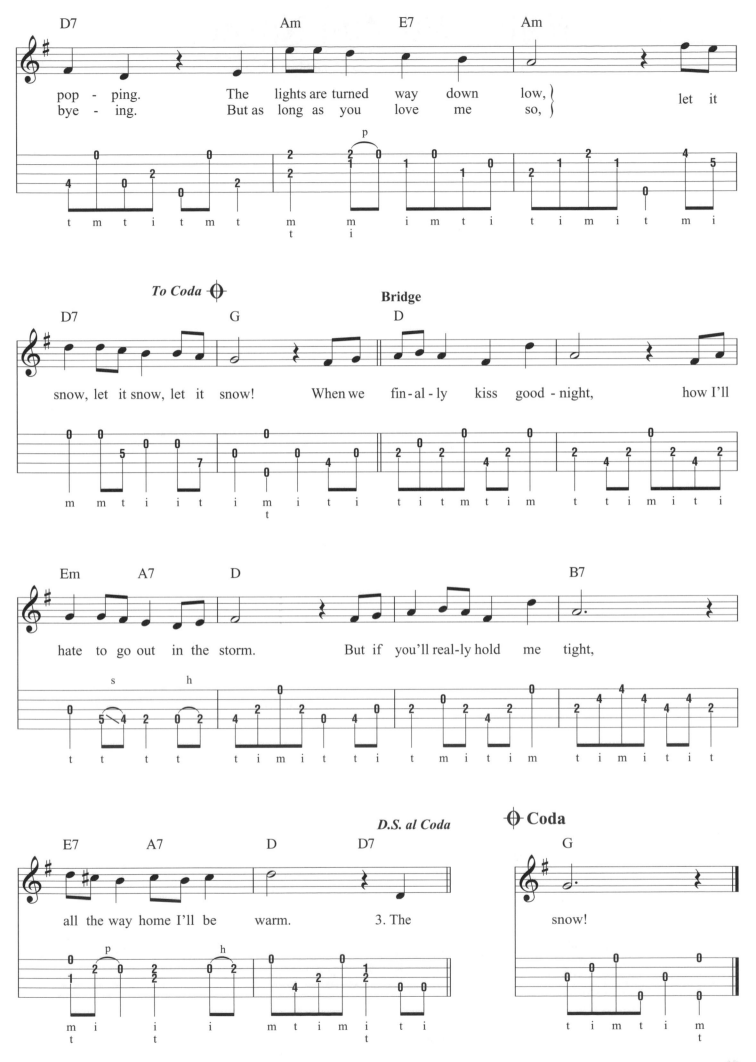

Mary, Did You Know?

Words and Music by Mark Lowry and Buddy Greene

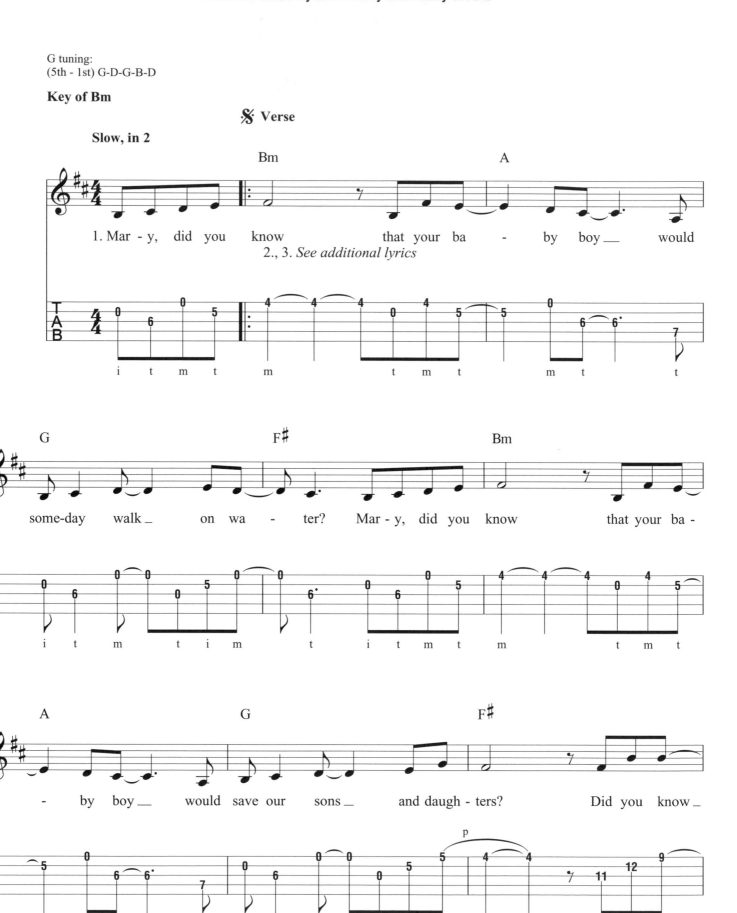

Additional Lyrics

2. Mary, did you know
   That your baby boy will give sight to a blind man?
   Mary, did you know
   That you baby boy will calm the storm with His hand?
   Did you know
   That your baby boy has walked where angels trod,
   When you kiss your little baby,
   You kiss the face of God?

3. Mary, did you know
   That your baby boy is Lord of all creation?
   Mary, did you know
   That your baby boy would one day rule the nations?
   Did you know
   That your baby boy is heaven's perfect Lamb?
   That sleeping Child you're holding is the great "I Am!"

Rockin' Around the Christmas Tree

Music and Lyrics by Johnny Marks

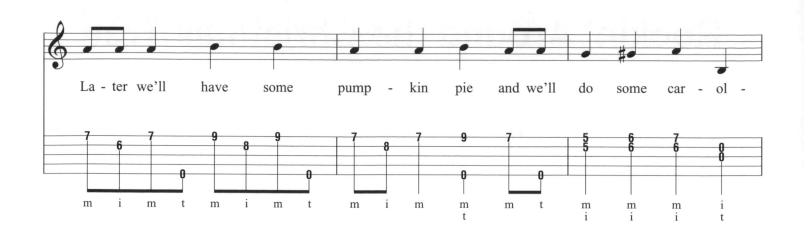

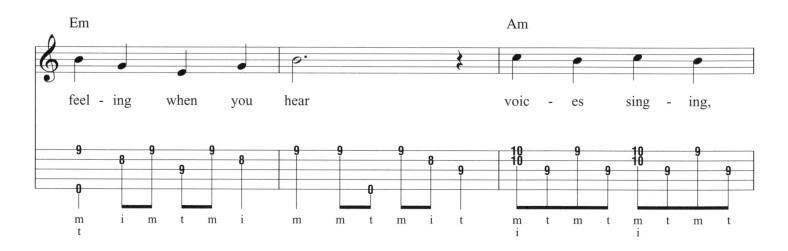

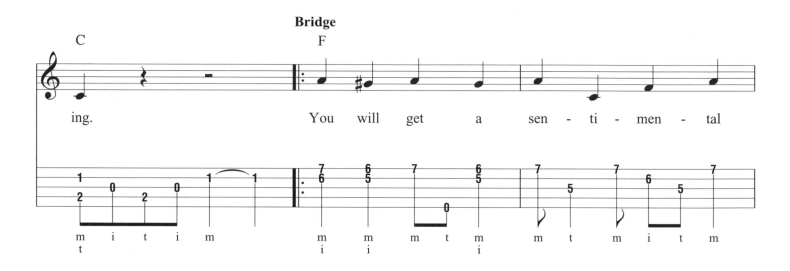

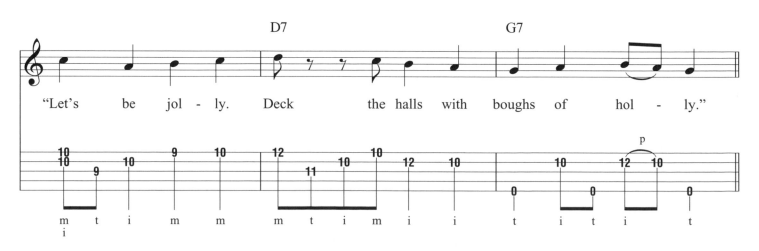

Merry Christmas, Darling

Words and Music by Richard Carpenter and Frank Pooler

G tuning:
(5th - 1st) G-D-G-B-D

Key of G

Intro
Freely

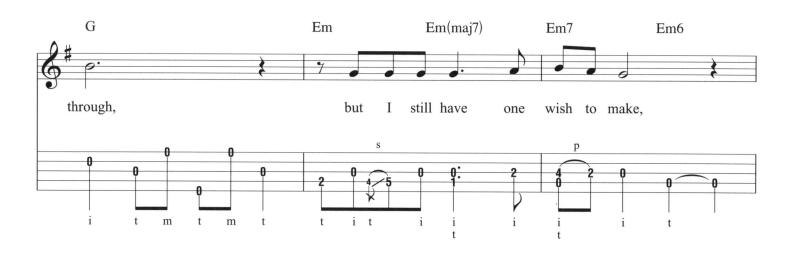

Verse
Moderately

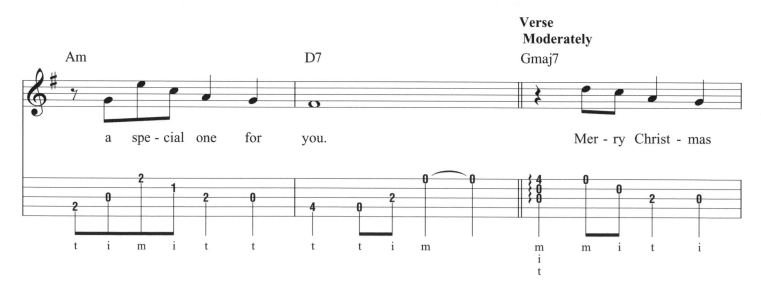

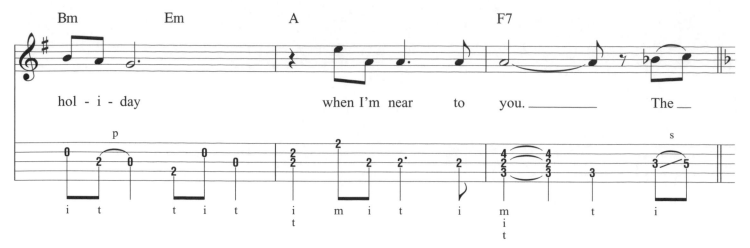

hol - i - day .... when I'm near to you. _____ The __

𝄋 **Bridge**

lights on my tree, I wish you could see. I wish it ev - 'ry -

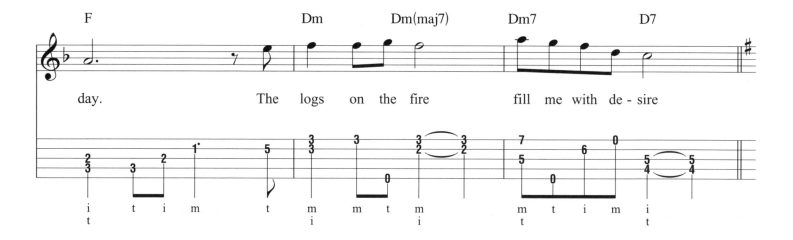

day. The logs on the fire fill me with de - sire

Key of G

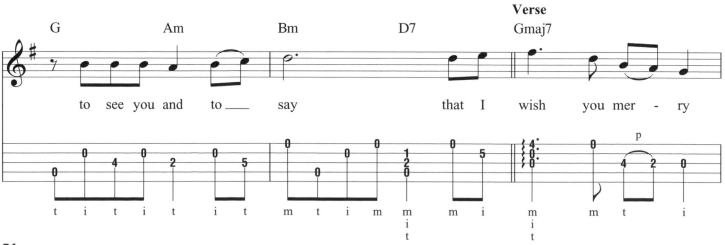

to see you and to ___ say that I wish you mer - ry

Verse

54

The Most Wonderful Time of the Year

Words and Music by Eddie Pola and George Wyle

G tuning:
(5th - 1st) G-D-G-B-D

Key of G

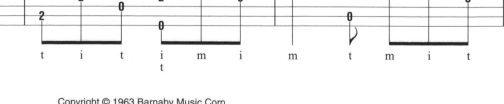

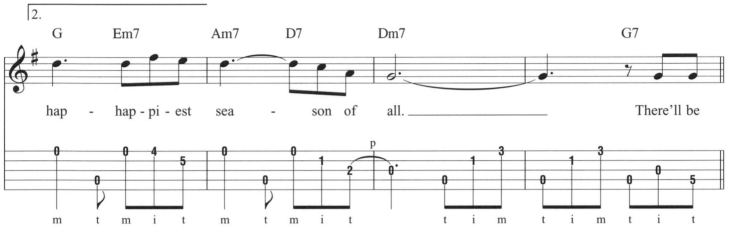

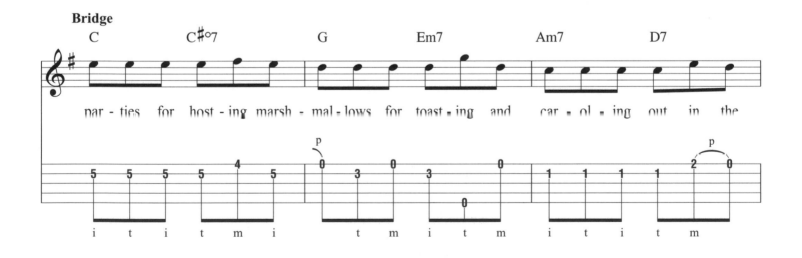

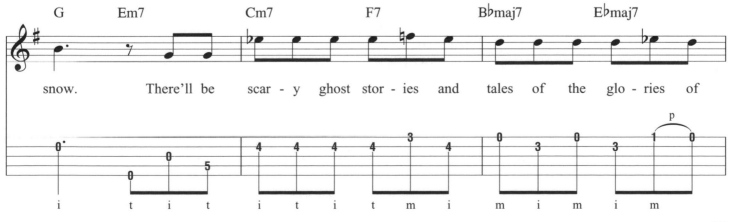

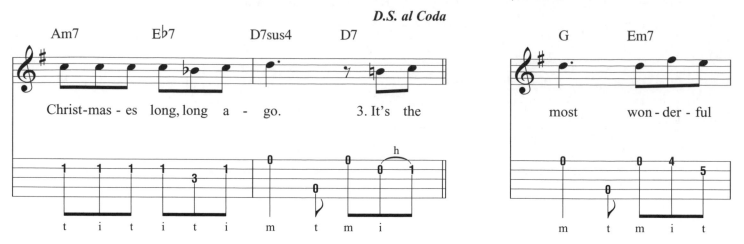

D.S. al Coda

Christ-mas - es long, long a - go.   3. It's the   most   won - der - ful

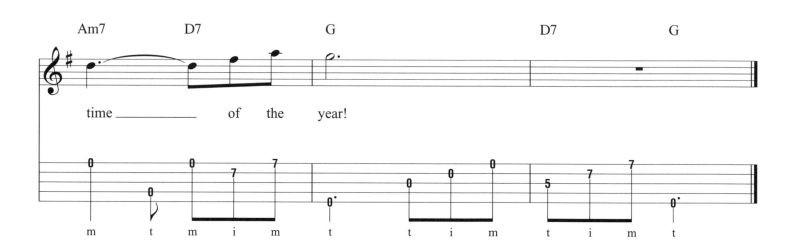

time _____ of the   year!

Additional Lyrics

2. It's the hap-happiest season of all,
   With those holiday greetings
   And gay happy meetings
   When friends come to call.
   It's the hap-happiest season of all.

3. It's the most wonderful time of the year.
   There'll be much mistletoeing
   And hearts will be glowing
   When loved ones are near.
   It's the most wonderful time of the year!

Rudolph the Red-Nosed Reindeer

Music and Lyrics by Johnny Marks

G tuning:
(5th - 1st) G-D-G-B-D

Key of C
Intro
Freely

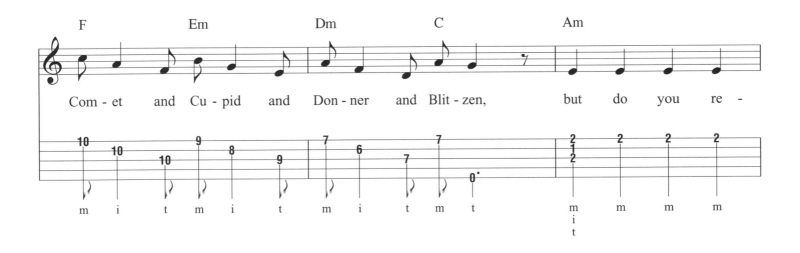

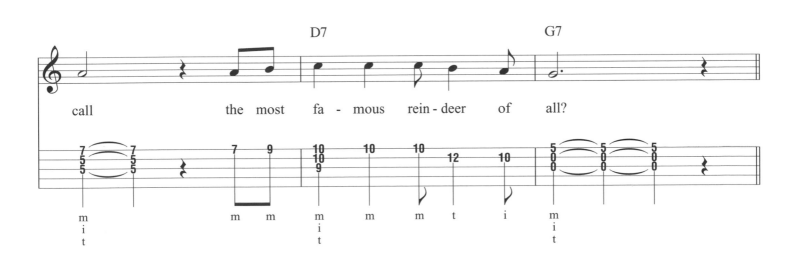

Silver Bells

from the Paramount Picture THE LEMON DROP KID
Words and Music by Jay Livingston and Ray Evans

G tuning:
(5th - 1st) G-D-G-B-D

Key of D

Verse

Slowly

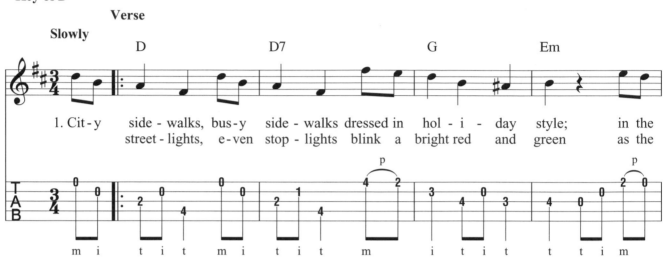

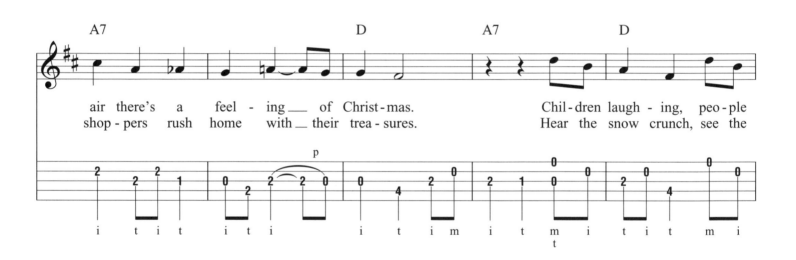

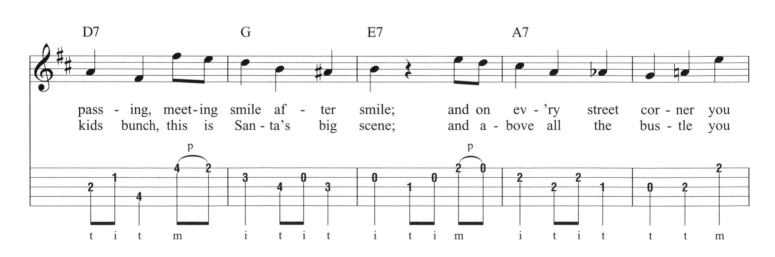

Sleigh Ride

Music by Leroy Anderson
Words by Mitchell Parish

G tuning:
(5th - 1st) G-D-G-B-D

Key of C
Intro
Moderately, in 2

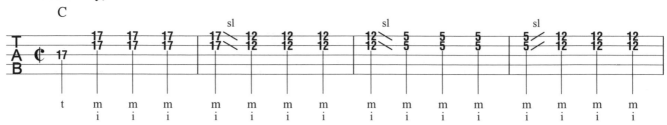

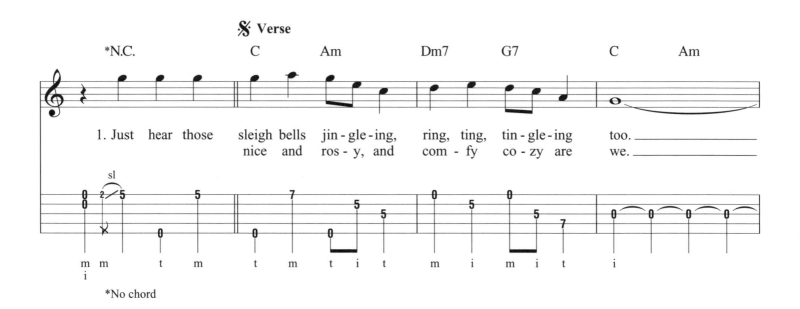

1. Just hear those sleigh bells jin-gle-ing, ring, ting, tin-gle-ing too. ___
   nice and ros-y, and com-fy co-zy are we. ___

*No chord

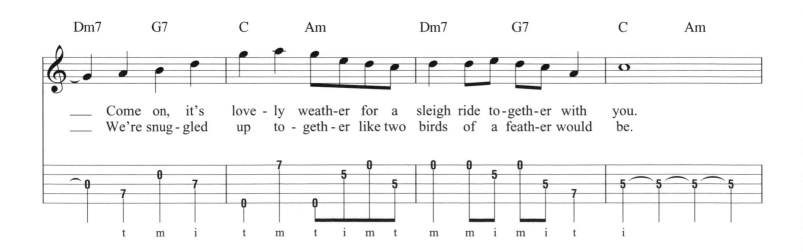

Come on, it's love-ly weath-er for a sleigh ride to-geth-er with you.
We're snug-gled up to-geth-er like two birds of a feath-er would be.

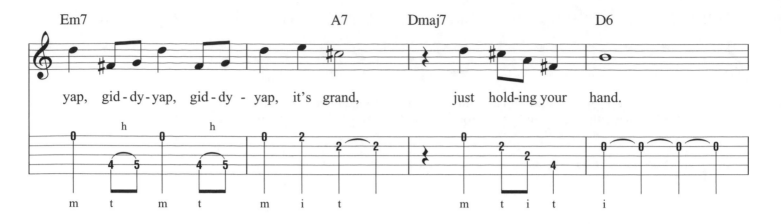

D.S. al Coda 1

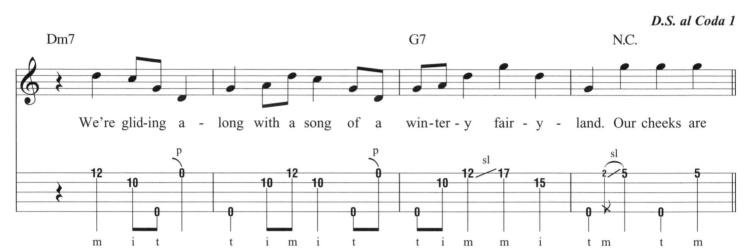

$\oplus$ **Coda 1**

Bridge

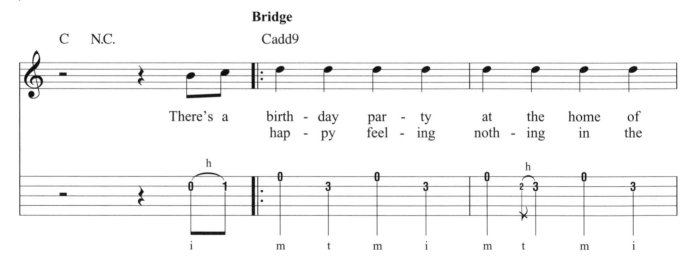

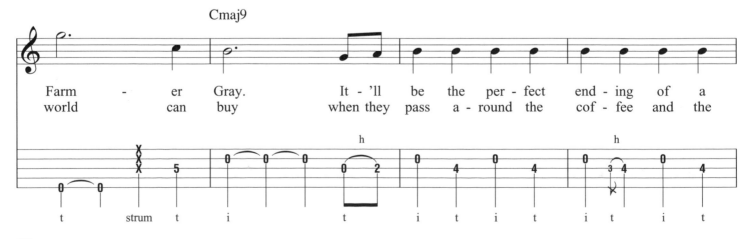

per - fect day.   We'll be sing-ing the songs we love to sing with-
pump - kin pie.   It-'ll near-ly be like a pic-ture print by

out a sin-gle stop,   at the fire - place while we
Cur - ri - er and

watch the chest - nuts pop.   Pop! Pop! Pop! There's a

Ives.   These won-der-ful things are the things we re -

Santa Claus Is Comin' to Town

Words by Haven Gillespie
Music by J. Fred Coots

G tuning:
(5th - 1st) G-D-G-B-D

Key of G

Verse
Moderately, in 2

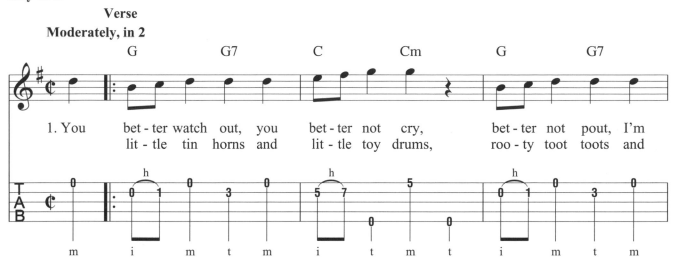

1. You bet-ter watch out, you bet-ter not cry, bet-ter not pout, I'm
   lit-tle tin horns and lit-tle toy drums, roo-ty toot toots and

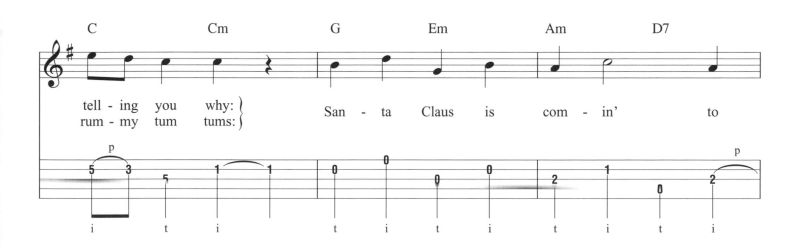

tell-ing you why: }
rum-my tum tums: }
San - ta Claus is com - in' to

Verse

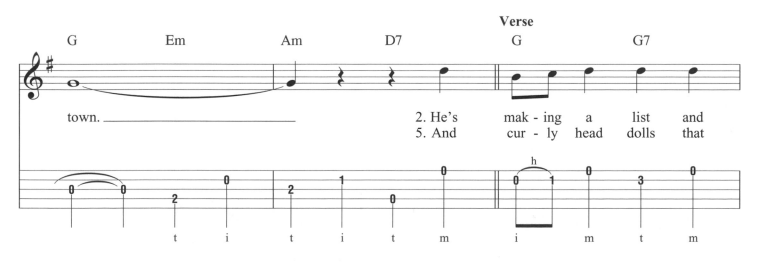

town. _____

2. He's mak-ing a list and
5. And cur-ly head dolls that

White Christmas

from the Motion Picture Irving Berlin's HOLIDAY INN

Words and Music by Irving Berlin

G tuning:
(5th - 1st) G-D-G-B-D

Key of G

Verse
Slow

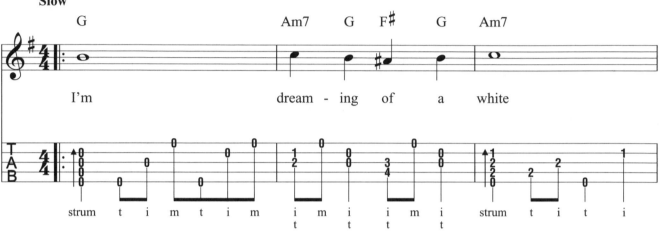

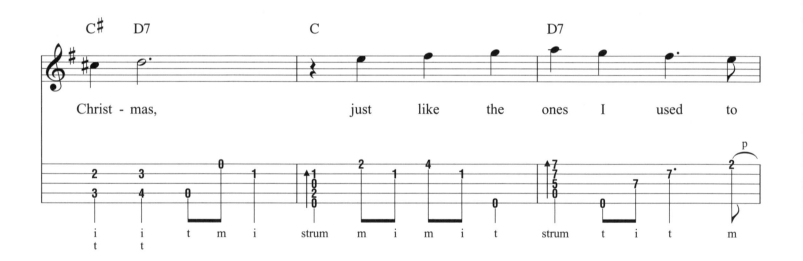

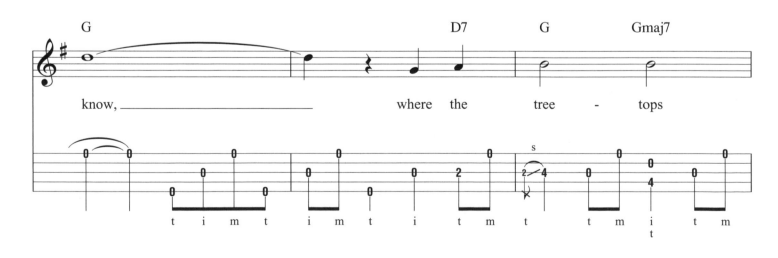

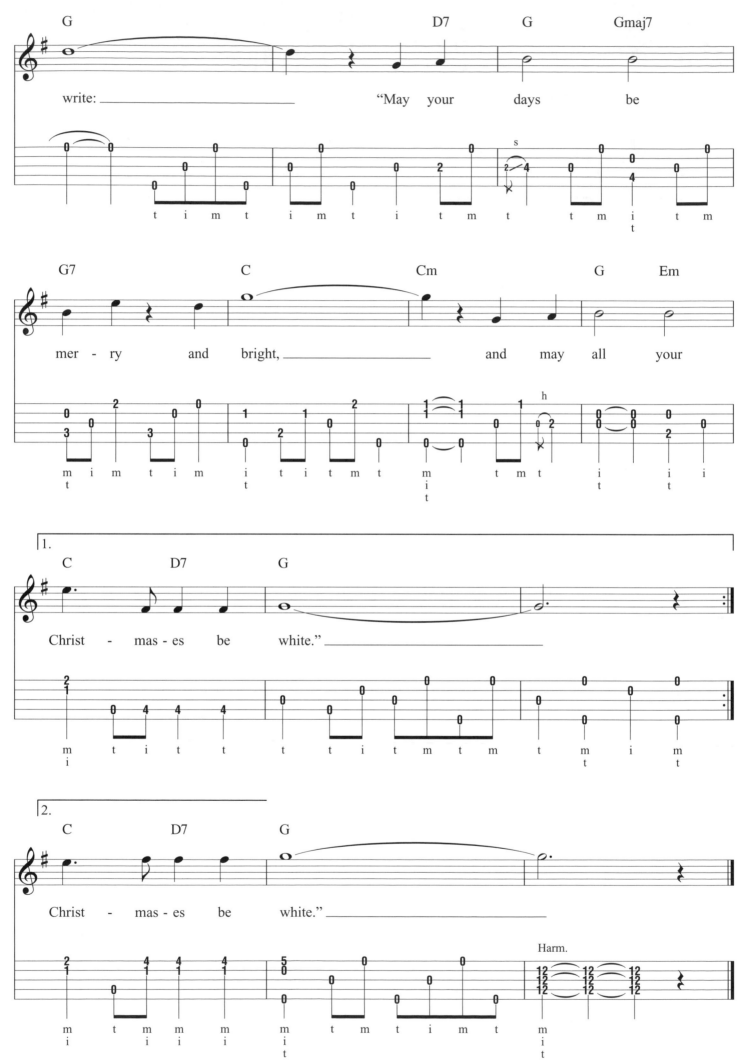

Winter Wonderland

Words by Dick Smith
Music by Felix Bernard

G tuning:
(5th - 1st) G-D-G-B-D

Key of C

Verse

Moderately

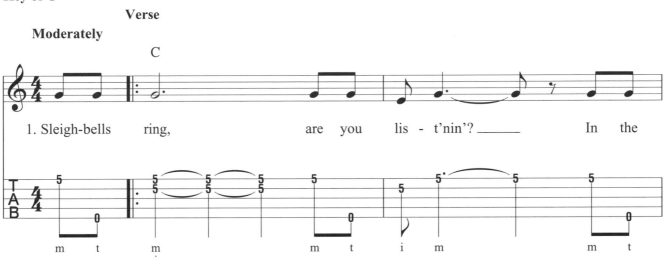

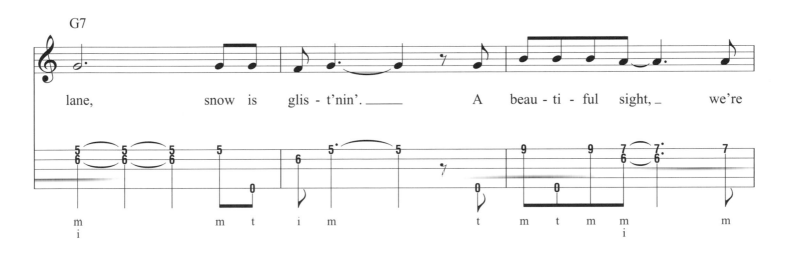

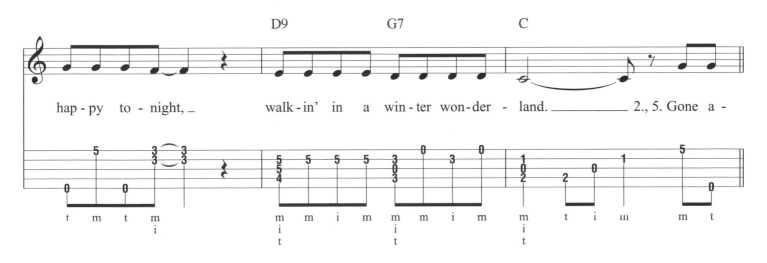

BANJO NOTATION LEGEND

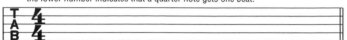

TABLATURE graphically represents the banjo fingerboard. Each horizontal line represents a string, and each number represents a fret.

Strings:
1 D
2 B
3 G
4 D
5 G

4th string, 2nd fret

1st & 2nd strings open, played together

TIME SIGNATURE:
The upper number indicates the number of beats per measure, the lower number indicates that a quarter note gets one beat.

CUT TIME:
Each note's time value should be cut in half. As a result, the music will be played twice as fast as it is written.

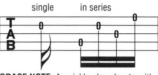

QUARTER NOTE:
time value = 1 beat

EIGHTH NOTES:
time value = 1/2 beat each

single   in series

SIXTEENTH NOTES:
time value = 1/4 beat each

single   in series

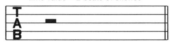

DOTTED QUARTER NOTE:
time value = 1 1/2 beat

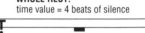

TIE: Pick the 1st note only, then let it sustain for the combined time value.

TRIPLET: Three notes played in the same time normally occupied by two notes of the same time value.

GRACE NOTE: A quickly played note with no time value of its own. The grace note and the note following it only occupy the time value of the second note.

RITARD: A gradual slowing of the tempo or speed of the song.

QUARTER REST:
time value = 1 beat of silence

EIGHTH REST:
time value = 1/2 beat of silence

HALF REST:
time value = 2 beats of silence

WHOLE REST:
time value = 4 beats of silence

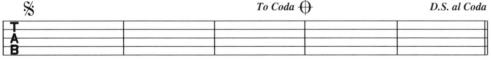

ENDINGS: When a repeated section has a first and second ending, play the first ending only the first time and play the second ending only the second time.

1.   2.

REPEAT SIGNS: Play the music between the repeat signs two times.

D.S. AL CODA:
Play through the music until you complete the measure labeled *"D.S. al Coda,"* then go back to the sign (𝄋). Then play until you complete the measure labeled *"To Coda ⊕,"* then skip to the section labeled *"⊕ Coda."*

𝄋   *To Coda* ⊕   *D.S. al Coda*   ⊕ *Coda*

HAMMER-ON: Strike the first (lower) note with one finger, then sound the higher note (on the same string) with another finger by fretting it without picking.

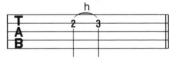

PULL-OFF: Place both fingers on the notes to be sounded. Strike the first note and without picking, pull the finger off to sound the second (lower) note.

SLIDE UP: Strike the first note and then slide the same fret-hand finger up to the second note. The second note is not struck.

SLIDE DOWN: Strike the first note and then slide the same fret-hand finger down to the second note. The second note is not struck.

HALF-STEP CHOKE: Strike the note and bend the string up 1/2 step.

WHOLE-STEP CHOKE: Strike the note and bend the string up one step.

NATURAL HARMONIC: Strike the note while the fret-hand lightly touches the string directly over the fret indicated.

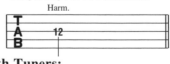

BRUSH: Play the notes of the chord indicated by quickly rolling them from bottom to top.

Scruggs/Keith Tuners:

HALF-TWIST UP: Strike the note, twist tuner up 1/2 step, and continue playing.

HALF-TWIST DOWN: Strike the note, twist tuner down 1/2 step, and continue playing.

WHOLE-TWIST UP: Strike the note, twist tuner up one step, and continue playing.

WHOLE-TWIST DOWN: Strike the note, twist tuner down one step, and continue playing.

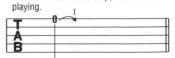

Right Hand Fingerings

t = thumb   i = index finger   m = middle finger

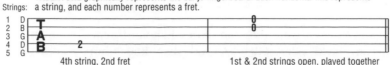

Hal Leonard Banjo Play-Along Series

HAL•LEONARD® BANJO PLAY-ALONG

AUDIO ACCESS INCLUDED

INCLUDES TAB

The Banjo Play-Along Series will help you play your favorite songs quickly and easily with incredible backing tracks to help you sound like a bona fide pro! Just follow the banjo tab, listen to the demo track on the CD or online audio to hear how the banjo should sound, and then play along with the separate backing tracks. The CD is playable on any CD player and also is enhanced so Mac and PC users can adjust the recording to any tempo without changing the pitch! Books with online audio also include PLAYBACK+ options such as looping and tempo adjustments. Each Banjo Play-Along pack features eight cream of the crop songs.

1. BLUEGRASS
Ashland Breakdown • Deputy Dalton • Dixie Breakdown • Hickory Hollow • I Wish You Knew • I Wonder Where You Are Tonight • Love and Wealth • Salt Creek.
00102585 Book/CD Pack........................$14.99

2. COUNTRY
East Bound and Down • Flowers on the Wall • Gentle on My Mind • Highway 40 Blues • If You've Got the Money (I've Got the Time) • Just Because • Take It Easy • You Are My Sunshine.
00105278 Book/CD Pack........................$14.99

3. FOLK/ROCK HITS
Ain't It Enough • The Cave • Forget the Flowers • Ho Hey • Little Lion Man • Live and Die • Switzerland • Wagon Wheel.
00119867 Book/CD Pack........................$14.99

4. OLD-TIME CHRISTMAS
Away in a Manger • Hark! the Herald Angels Sing • Jingle Bells • Joy to the World • O Holy Night • O Little Town of Bethlehem • Silent Night • We Wish You a Merry Christmas.
00119889 Book/CD Pack........................$14.99

5. PETE SEEGER
Blue Skies • Get up and Go • If I Had a Hammer (The Hammer Song) • Kisses Sweeter Than Wine • Mbube (Wimoweh) • Sailing Down My Golden River • Turn! Turn! Turn! (To Everything There Is a Season) • We Shall Overcome.
00129699 Book/CD Pack........................$17.99

6. SONGS FOR BEGINNERS
Bill Cheatham • Black Mountain Rag • Cripple Creek • Grandfather's Clock • John Hardy • Nine Pound Hammer • Old Joe Clark • Will the Circle Be Unbroken.
00139751 Book/CD Pack........................$14.99

7. BLUEGRASS GOSPEL
Cryin' Holy unto the Lord • How Great Thou Art • I Saw the Light • I'll Fly Away • I'll Have a New Life • Man in the Middle • Turn Your Radio On • Wicked Path of Sin.
00147594 Book/Online Audio $14.99

8. CELTIC BLUEGRASS
Billy in the Low Ground • Cluck Old Hen • Devil's Dream • Fisher's Hornpipe • Little Maggie • Over the Waterfall • The Red Haired Boy • Soldier's Joy.
00160077 Book/Online Audio $14.99

www.halleonard.com

1216

GREAT BANJO PUBLICATIONS
FROM HAL LEONARD

Hal Leonard Banjo Method – Second Edition
by Mac Robertson, Robbie Clement, Will Schmid
This innovative method teaches 5-string banjo bluegrass style using a carefully paced approach that keeps beginners playing great songs *while learning*. Book 1 covers easy chord strums, tablature, right-hand rolls, hammer-ons, slides and pull-offs, and more. Book 2 includes solos and licks, fiddle tunes, back-up, capo use, and more.

00699500 Book 1 Book Only $7.99
00695101 Book 1 Book/Online Audio $16.99
00699502 Book 2 Book Only $7.99

Banjo Aerobics
A 50-Week Workout Program for Developing, Improving and Maintaining Banjo Technique
by Michael Bremer
Take your banjo playing to the next level with this fantastic daily resource, providing a year's worth of practice material with a two-week vacation. The accompanying audio includes demo tracks for all the examples in the book to reinforce how the banjo should sound.

00113734 Book/Online Audio $19.99

Banjo Chord Finder
This extensive reference guide covers over 2,800 banjo chords, including four of the most commonly used tunings. Thirty different chord qualities are covered for each key, and each chord quality is presented in two different voicings. Also includes a lesson on chord construction and a fingerboard chart of the banjo neck!

00695741 9 x 12.. $6.99
00695742 6 x 9.. $6.99

Banjo Scale Finder
by Chad Johnson
Learn to play scales on the banjo with this comprehensive yet easy-to-use book. It contains more than 1,300 scale diagrams for the most often-used scales and modes, including multiple patterns for each scale. Also includes a lesson on scale construction and a fingerboard chart of the banjo neck.

00695780 9 x 12.. $9.99
00695783 6 x 9.. $6.99

The Beatles for Banjo
18 of the Fab Four's finest for five string banjo! Includes: Across the Universe • Blackbird • A Hard Day's Night • Here Comes the Sun • Hey Jude • Let It Be • She Loves You • Strawberry Fields Forever • Ticket to Ride • Yesterday • and more.

00700813 ....$14.99

Fretboard Roadmaps
by Fred Sokolow
This handy book/with online audio will get you playing all over the banjo fretboard in any key! You'll learn to: increase your chord, scale and lick vocabulary • play chord-based licks, moveable major and blues scales, melodic scales and first-position major scales • and much more! The audio includes 51 demonstrations of the exercises.

00695358 Book/Online Audio................................... $14.95

O Brother, Where Art Thou?
Banjo tab arrangements of 12 bluegrass/folk songs from this Grammy-winning album. Includes: The Big Rock Candy Mountain • Down to the River to Pray • I Am a Man of Constant Sorrow • I Am Weary (Let Me Rest) • I'll Fly Away • In the Jailhouse Now • Keep on the Sunny Side • You Are My Sunshine • and more, plus lyrics and a banjo notation legend.

00699528 Banjo Tablature... $14.99

Earl Scruggs and the 5-String Banjo
Earl Scruggs' legendary method has helped thousands of banjo players get their start. It features everything you need to know to start playing, even how to build your own banjo! Topics covered include: Scruggs tuners • how to read music • chords • how to read tablature • anatomy of Scruggs-style picking • exercises in picking • 44 songs • biographical notes • and more! The CD features Earl Scruggs playing and explaining over 60 examples!

00695764 Book Only.. $22.99
00695765 Book/CD Pack $34.99

The Tony Trischka Collection
59 authentic transcriptions by Tony Trischka, one of the world's best banjo pickers and instructors. Includes: Blown Down Wall • China Grove • Crossville Breakdown • Heartlands • Hill Country • Kentucky Bullfight • A Robot Plane Flies over Arkansas • and more. Features an introduction by Béla Fleck, plus Tony's comments on each song. Transcriptions are in tab only.

00699063 Banjo Tablature... $19.95

The Ultimate Banjo Songbook
A great collection of banjo classics: Alabama Jubilee • Bye Bye Love • Duelin' Banjos • The Entertainer • Foggy Mountain Breakdown • Great Balls of Fire • Lady of Spain • Orange Blossom Special • (Ghost) Riders in the Sky • Rocky Top • San Antonio Rose • Tennessee Waltz • UFO-TOFU • You Are My Sunshine • and more.

00699565 Book/Online Audio................................... $27.50

Prices, contents, and availability subject to change without notice.

Visit Hal Leonard online at **www.halleonard.com**

0717